The Holy Land Bible Study

The Holy Land Bible Study

Stop! Look! Listen!

(Volume 1)
For those who have been to the Holy Land,
are planning a trip to the Holy Land,
or
are dreaming about a trip to the Holy Land

JEANNE SANT

JEANNE SANT
PRESENTED BY SAMANNA MINISTRIES

The Holy Land Bible Study: Stop! Look! Listen! (volume 1)
Jeanne Sant
Samanna Ministries
Knoxville, TN
Copyright 2015 Jeanne Sant
Unless otherwise noted, all scripture references are taken from NKJV

http://www.wostudyhall.gmail.com

ISBN: 1508667985
ISBN 13: 9781508667988

Dedication

This book is dedicated to all the friends and family with whom I have had the blessing of traveling to the Holy Land and also to those with whom I have not yet. Maybe that is you!

We have traveled the Holy Land together many times.
In heat and cold, sun and rain.
    Even in the snow!
We have traveled by plane, bus, boat, tram, foot.
    Even by camel!
We have been "from Dan to Beersheba,"
From the blue Mediterranean,
    to the red clay of Petra.
From the bunkers cut in the Golan,
    to the tomb cut in Mount Moriah.
From the Temple Mount,
    to the top of Masada.
From Capernaum on the shores of the Sea of Galilee,
    to Ein Gedi on the shores of the Dead Sea.
From Bethlehem, where it all began,
    to Megiddo, where it will all end.
From the Eastern Gate,
    to the Western Wall.
From where the waters of Mount Hermon join the Jordan River,
    to the Red Sea at Elat.

From the horrors of the Holocaust Museum,
    to the quiet place where baby Jesus was born
We have sifted through ancient dirt in archaeological digs.
We have planted trees that will grow into great forests.
We have stood in the Knesset, where lawmakers protect the country.
We have explored the ruins of cities, an underground street, synagogues, homes, prisons, steps, pools, bunkers, Tels, theaters, cemeteries, stables, and even an ancient boat.
We are always amazed and in wonderment as our lives are changed with each trip.
We have truly been blessed.

Introduction

I AM WRITING this book primarily for those who are preparing to visit the Holy Land. At the moment, I am about a month away from my next trip. I began to write these studies for my group in order to prepare them for what they will be seeing, and the project has developed into a book.

I remember what it was like to visit the Holy Land for the first time. I kept saying things like "I wish I had studied this site" and "I wish I knew the importance of this site." I want to help others avoid saying this.

For those who have been to the Holy Land, this study will help you remember all that you saw. Just writing this study has filled me with joy and excitement. I relived every site and felt truly blessed. I hope you will too.

And for those who are considering a visit to the Holy Land, this study should give you an idea of what you might see.

The following is a brief overview of some of the sites that tourists to the Holy Land visit. Each tour group, each tour guide are unique. Not all trips are carbon copies of the previous trip. Out of all the sites, why did I choose these for Volume 1? I selected sites that were not so well known, as well as the most common sites. Few tourists will understand the significance of the Church of Saint Peter in Gallicantu or the gates of Jerusalem, but most travelers will be familiar with the Jordan River. There are enough sites to write two or three Bible studies! Hmm...

Reasons to Travel to the Holy Land A to Z

YOU HAVE THE time. You can manage the money. What are you waiting for? This may be the opportune time to visit all the sites of the Holy Land that you have read about in scripture. God calls Israel the *Holy Land* and the *land of milk and honey,* but He also calls it the *glorious land.* Who wouldn't want to see it?

In 1991, at the young age of fifty-three, I made my first trip to Israel. I found out that everything people say about traveling to the Holy Land is true:

- It changes your life. You will literally never be the same. You will be changed spiritually after you walk in the very land where Jesus walked.
- It makes scripture come alive.
- There is no place on earth like Israel; the sights, sounds, and emotions are like nothing else you have ever experienced.
- As a pastor or teacher, you will gain deep insights that will change every aspect of your study and teaching.

After the first trip, I did not return until 1996. Little did I know that after this second trip, I would return again and again—sometimes twice a year—and plan to go back again in 2016! I guess I will continue to return as long as my health permits the travel.

One scene is often repeated on my trips. When we sail on the Sea of Galilee, at least one older man—usually a pastor—will begin to cry. His comment is always the same: "Why didn't I do this when I was younger? It would have made my ministry more powerful."

This is a trip of a lifetime.

Here are reasons, from *A* to *Z*, for you to visit the Holy Land.

A—This sight was stunning to me. I still can't get it out of my mind: Armageddon (Megiddo). See where scripture prophesized that end-time events will occur. From the cliffs of the ancient city of Megiddo, look across the fertile, green, broad valley in northern Israel where the end-time battle, predicted in Ezekiel and Revelation, will take place. "A" is also for: participate in an archaeological dig.

B—View Bethlehem. This is the famous site of Jesus's birth and the location of the story of Ruth and Boaz. Visit the ruins of Beit She'an, where the bodies of Saul and his sons hung on the city walls after their deaths.

C—See the town of Cana, where Jesus performed his first miracle of changing water into wine. Walk through the ruins of the city Chorazin, one of the three cities that Jesus cursed.

D—Visit the shrinking Dead Sea. Somewhere along the shores are the sites of Sodom and Gomorrah, Ein Gedi (where David fled several times from Saul), and the mountain ruins of Masada.

E—See the Eastern Gate, where Jesus entered Jerusalem on the back of a colt and where scripture indicates Jesus will return. (No, you cannot walk through this gate.)

F—Visit the site of the feeding of the multitude.

G—You will experience a variety of emotions as you visit the empty Garden Tomb. "He is no longer here—He has risen!" Drive over the Golan Heights and get an up-close view of Syria and Jordan. "G" is also for gates: walk through many of the ancient gates of Jerusalem mentioned in scripture.

H—Step atop the Temple Mount, where God resided in the Holy of Holies. See the Hula Valley in northern Israel. It is a swamp that was drained and is now a major agricultural area.

I—Drive through the land of the twelve tribes of Israel.

J—Actually stand in the city of Jerusalem, the center of the spiritual world for Christians, Jews, and Muslims, as well as the center of unrest in the political world today. This is the "City of God," and you will be there!

K—Tour the recently uncovered ruins of King David's palace, where he looked down at Bathsheba as she bathed on her roof.

L—Drive through "the land flowing with milk and honey." See the many farms and herds of livestock that dot the land.

M—View the Mount of Transfiguration. Visit the Mount of Beatitudes, where Jesus gave one of His most studied teachings. See Mount Tabor and Mount Gilboa.

N—Drive through the streets of Nazareth, the boyhood city of Jesus. Visit the Nazareth Village and see how Jesus lived.

O—Walk down the Palm Sunday Road to the Mount of Olives and into the garden of Gethsemane, where Jesus went to pray before His arrest. Scripture says Jesus will return and place His feet on the Mount of Olives to usher in the millennium.

P—You will be in the Promised Land of the patriarchs. You will see the stone inscription at Caesarea Maritime that actually names Pontius Pilate, proving for all the skeptics that there was an official named Pilate who lived during the time of Jesus.

Q—Visit Qumran. View the caves where handwritten portions of scripture were found in 1948, assuring us that what we hold in our hands as scripture today is authentic.

R—Be baptized in the Jordan River. "R" is also for: ride a camel.

S—The area around the Sea of Galilee has numerous important sites. Jesus made His home in Capernaum, where He attended synagogue and performed the majority of His of healings and miracles. Visit the museum of the "Jesus Boat," the unearthed skeleton of a boat dating to the time of Jesus. Study at the ruins of the home where the healing of Peter's mother-in-law took place. Ride a boat out to the center of the Sea of Galilee and stop where Jesus walked on water.

T—Tour the Temple Mount, where Anna and Simeon recognized the infant as the Messiah, where young Jesus went to teach the teachers, and where He overturned the tables of the businessmen, selling for profit. Today the Temple Mount is the center of all of the fighting in the Middle East. See it firsthand! Also located on the Temple Mount are the world-famous Dome of the Rock and Al-Aqsa Mosque.

U—Visit the traditional site of the Upper Room, where Jesus and the disciples celebrated the Last Supper.

V—Walk the Via Dolorosa and stop at the traditional fourteen points along the path Jesus took with the cross.

W—Pray at the Western (Wailing) Wall, the spiritual center for the Jewish religion.

X—*X* marks the spot. Israel is the center of the world, not only spiritually, but politically as well. (Sorry, there is just no *X*!)

Y—Visit a recently opened site along the *Yardin* (the Hebrew term for the Jordan River), just north of the Dead Sea, considered by many scholars to be the actual site of the baptism of Jesus. You will be standing just fifty yards from the country of Jordan.

Z—Walk Mount Zion, where so many biblical events took place.

And there is so much more! This is just a short list of what you will see!

Glossary of Terms Tourists Need to Know

Mount/Mountain

A MOUNTAIN IN Israel may not be what most of us think of as a mountain. The Smoky Mountains are mountains! The highest mountain of the Smoky Mountains, Clingmans Dome, rises 6,643 feet. Compare this with the mountains of Israel:

The Mount of Olives rises 2,710 feet at its highest point.
Mount Zion, west of the Temple Mount, rises 2,510 feet.
Mount Moriah, the Temple Mount, rises 2,440 feet.
Mount Tabor rises 1,843 feet.
Mount Gilboa rises 508 feet.
Mount of Beatitudes rises 410 feet.

The Four Quarters of Jerusalem

The city of Jerusalem is divided into "quarters," Here ethnic/religious groups of people tend to inhabit a specific neighborhood. There are Jewish, Christian, Armenian, and Arab (or Muslim) quarters.

River

Due to the shortage of water and the diversion of water from rivers to irrigate farms, a river in Israel is more like a stream in the United States.

Most of these rivers are not very wide. It would be easy to swim or walk to the opposite side. Don't expect to see a large river.

Consider the following comparisons:

The Jordan River is 155 miles long. The Mississippi River is 2,340 miles long.

The Kishon River is 44 miles long. The Tennessee River is 651 miles long.

The Yarmuk River is also 44 miles long. The Rio Grande is 1,896 miles long.

The Dan River is 13 miles long. The Duck River in Tennessee is 284 miles long.

Sea

In Israel, the word *sea* doesn't refer to an enormous body of water, i.e. the Sea of Japan or the Caspian Sea. The reference to 'sea' in Israel refers to a much smaller body of water.

The Sea of Galilee is a lake thirteen miles long and eight miles wide. It is also called the Sea of Chinnereth, Lake of Gennesaret, or Lake Tiberias.

The Dead Sea (also named the Salt Sea in the Old Testament) is not a sea, but it is dead. Water flows into the Dead Sea from the Jordan River, but it has no outlet. The water is evaporated by the desert sun, which increases the concentration of minerals from the soil and brings the saline content to 25 percent. Nothing lives in this water.

Tel

Israel has Tel Megiddo, Tel Dan, and many other similarly named places. So what is a Tel? In Hebrew, a *Tel* refers to a hill or mound that is made up of layers of ancient ruins of a city. When a city was overrun by enemies, it was razed, and a new city was built upon the stones, rocks, and bricks of the previous city, like a stack of pancakes. For example, Tel Megiddo has at least seven civilizations built one upon the other.

Via

The word *Via* means "way" or "road." For example, *Via Maris* means "way of the sea." It was the main route for caravans traveling along the coast from north to south (from Egypt to Damascus.

Via Dolorosa (the route Jesus took as He carried the cross on the way to Golgotha) means "way of pain."

Contents

1

❧

Geography: Israel in the World

THE FOLLOWING THREE quizzes will test your knowledge of the basics of the geography of Israel. Each of these quizzes will be repeated in the Appendix so that those who have traveled to the Holy Land can test what they have learned, upon their return home.

Israel in the World: Pre-trip

How long would it take you to locate Israel on a world map?

Name the oceans and seas bordering Israel (not including the Dead Sea).

Name the country south of Israel.

Name the countries east of Israel.

Name the countries north of Israel.

What is the capital of Israel as recognized by the major nations of the world?

What is the capital of Israel as designated by the Israeli government?

Geography of the Land: Pre-trip

For those who have traveled to Israel, take the post-trip quiz, which is located in the Appendix.

Draw a basic outline of Israel. Locate and label the following:

1. Mediterranean Sea
2. Sea of Galilee
3. Jordan River
4. Dead Sea
5. Jerusalem
6. Capernaum
7. Bethlehem
8. Nazareth

Geography of the Sea of Galilee: Pre-trip

For those who have traveled to Israel, take the post-trip quiz, which is located in the Appendix.

The Sea of Galilee was the location of many of the miracles of Jesus. Draw a basic outline of the Sea of Galilee. Locate and label the following:

1. Tiberias
2. Migdol
3. Capernaum
4. Site of Sermon on the Mount
5. Golan Heights
6. Site of the feeding of the multitude
7. Site of the healing of the demoniac man (swine into sea)
8. Inlet of water into the Sea of Galilee
9. The outflow site into the Jordan River
10. Any other sites that interest you

2

Every Step You Take:
The Tribes of Israel

RECORD YOUR STUDY resources here.

From memory, what do you already know about the twelve tribes of Israel? In reality, there were fourteen tribes. Why were there fourteen tribes?

Why Study the Twelve Tribes of Israel?

Why bother to study the Holy Land through the twelve tribes? With all the other important sites we will see, why study tribes (that no longer even officially exist) at all? Because every day you are in Israel, every step you take, will be in a specific plot of land allocated by God to a specific tribe.

We will travel over the land of most of the tribes. God calls only one nation His chosen people, and only one geographical location is called the Holy Land. His land. The tribes were the nation. The tribal allotment of land made up the Holy Land. Each day of your trip, as you travel through the north, east, south, and west parts of the Holy Land, you will be in a part of land that was allocated to the tribes.

The tribes were important to the workings of God's plan of redemption. This should be important to us. Jacob was the father of all the tribes. Leah, Rachel, and two slave girls were the mothers of the tribes. The tribe of Levi consisted of the priests. Ruth from Moab married Boaz from the tribe of Judah. This was the beginning of the line of King David. Jesus was born in Bethlehem to the tribe of Judah, which gave proof to His claim of being the promised Messiah from the line of David. Salvation came through the line of Judah. And so much more.

What is a tribe?

Stop!

From memory, name and write a summary statement about each of the fourteen tribes. Who were the leaders? What did they accomplish? How did they fail?

Find a map of the locations of the tribes of Israel. Locate the Sea of Galilee, the Dead Sea, Nazareth, Bethlehem, the Jordan River, and Jerusalem. Which tribe had been allocated the land for each of these well-known sites?

Look!

The following is a listing of a few familiar references to the tribes:

The tribe of Judah was the tribe of Jesus.

The tribe of Benjamin was the tribe of Saul. All the men of Benjamin were killed, and husbands had to be found for the women. Paul said he was from the tribe of Benjamin.

The Tribe of Asher included Anna, the prophetess from Luke 2.

What other references do you remember?

The primary scriptures for the twelve tribes are listed below. Birth and genealogy:

> Gen. 29–30, 35:22–26, 46:8–27
> Exod.1:1–5
> Num. 1:20–54
> 1 Chron. 2–7
> Blessings of the sons and tribes by Jacob: Gen. 49
> Blessings of the sons and tribes by Moses: Deut. 33
> Camp position of the tribes around the Tabernacle: Num. 2:3–29, 7–1–88, 10:11–29
> Census: Num. 1:19+ and Num. 26:4+
> Land allotments for the tribes: Num. 34:19–28, Josh. 13–19
> Land allotment for the Levites: Josh. 21:4–8
> Military: 1 Chron. 12:24–38, 27:16–22
> Tribes in millennium: Ezek. 48

An in-depth study of the tribes teaches patterns, such as the place of the firstborn, headship, and roles. Many times, there is no specific reason given for God's actions, yet we see His divine pattern repeating itself. These patterns speak to us today in the life of the church and the family. God has roles for us as he did for the tribes. Through a study of the tribes, we will learn that our God is the God of order and organization.

Where are the tribes today? The answer is not within the scope of this lesson. Briefly, the tribal identification has been lost over the centuries because of the dispersion of people throughout the world. Ask a modern-day Jew which tribe he or she comes from, and he or she may look at you as if you were from Mars. There is some research indicating that several groups of people live outside of Israel but have kept their Jewish heritage and claim a Jewish bloodline. Research is ongoing.

In reality, there are no "lost tribes" to God. Scripture indicates that in the time of the tribulation, there will be 144,000 Jewish Evangelists, or twelve thousand men from every tribe (Rev. 7).

Listen!
Perhaps this study has fostered in you an interest in studying the tribes of Israel in depth.

What have you learned about God, His character, and the tribes that is applicable to your life today?

As you travel the land, remember that you are in the land allocated to one of God's tribes!

3

Jordan River

The Baptism of Jesus

Record your study sources here.

Stop!

Background Information

The Jordan River is formed by water flowing from three streams in the foothills of Mount Hermon in northern Israel. The melting snow from the peaks of Mount Hermon, descends into the Sea of Galilee, flowing sixty-five miles south to the Dead Sea. Agricultural run-off in the region has reduced the flow of the river some 90 percent, making it like a small stream in some places.

There are two baptismal sites.

The baptismal site that most people visit and are baptized at is located at the south end of the Sea of Galilee, where the out flow from the Sea begins the Jordan River. Called the Yardenit Baptismal Site, this location was built from funds provided by churches in the United States and provides a beautiful location, a changing area, gathering areas, and railings leading down into the river. Of course, all the tourist-shop amenities are there too! Built in 1981, this is the site where hundreds of thousands, if not millions, of visitors and pilgrims from all over the world have come, and continue to come, to be baptized. You will also have an opportunity to be baptized at this site.

Scripture indicates that Jesus was baptized further south, east of Jericho and Jerusalem. Today biblical scholars believe that the actual site of Jesus's baptism was just north of the Dead Sea, seventeen miles east of the city of Jericho. This site is known as Katzer el Yahud, or Qasr Al-Yahud. This is in the land that was allocated to the tribe of Benjamin.

Katzer el Yahud was closed to tourists until 2010. The Jordan River separates Israel from the nation of Jordan by just a few dozen feet at this site. Prior to a current peace agreement between Jordan and Israel, authorities acted with utmost concern for tourists and would not permit visitation to this site.

How close is this baptismal site to the country of Jordan? A person can stand on the banks of Jordan and have a conversation with someone standing on the banks of the river in Israel without having to raise his or her voice very loudly.

This site is considered to be the more likely site of the baptism of Jesus, based on the findings of ruins of an ancient Byzantine church on the banks of the eastern side of the Jordan River (the side of the river in Jordan). Inscriptions in the ruins of the church mark this as the primary location site of the baptisms of John the Baptist. Tourists visiting the country of Jordan may actually visit the ruins of this church.

At Katzer el Yahud, a beautiful site awaits the tourist. There is a covered, open-air gathering place for prayer and teaching. Few, if any, baptisms occur here.

Most groups traveling in the Holy Land visit both sites.

Look!

Refer to a map of the Holy Land. Start by looking in the back of your Bible. Study the following places:

- the area of the Sea of Galilee (some maps might even show Mount Hermon)
- the location of the outflow of water from the flow Sea of Galilee as it becomes the Jordan River
- the location of the country of Jordan
- the flow of the Jordan River from the Sea of Galilee to its ending at the Dead Sea
- the locations of Jericho and Jerusalem

Each of the four gospels recounts the baptism of Jesus. Which writers, if any, were present when John the Baptist baptized Jesus?

As a general overview, read the following accounts from Matthew, Mark, and Luke. (We will study the account in the Gospel of John.)

- Matt. 3:1–17
- Mark 1:1–12
- Luke 3:1–22

Begin to study the account of the baptism as written by John. Read John 1:6–8, 19–36.

Note any verses of particular interest to you or that you might want to research further.

Here are several lines you might want to study:

"Like a dove" (Vs 32). Was this a dove?

Who is referred to as "He who remained upon Him" (Vs 32)?

"I did not know Him" (Vs 33). How were Jesus and John related?

Who sent John?

Verses 31 and 33. Why did John not just say *baptize*? Why did he add the words "with water'?

What did John mean with the phrase "baptism with the Holy Spirit" (Vs 33b)?

What is the title given to Jesus in verse 34?

Katzer el Yahud has particular importance because not only was Jesus there, but God and the Holy Spirit were present. As you stand on the banks of the Jordan River at Bethabara (vs 29), remember that at this location, the Holy Spirit was present "like a dove," and Jesus was called the *Lamb*, His title that would be repeated again in the book of Revelation.

Also, as you stand at this site, also remember John the Baptist. His life and purpose had been foretold in Isaiah 40:3. Here in John 1, centuries later, it was fulfilled. John was not only a messenger, but a walking fulfilment of prophecy. What God promises shall come to pass.

Listen!

How can you apply this lesson to the following areas of your life today?

At work?

At home, with family, and spouse?

As you read the headlines in the news?

As you plan your ministry to the Lord?

For those who will be traveling to the Holy Land, remember that this event took place on the banks of the Jordan River, and you will stand there! How does that make you feel? What are you thinking?

For those who have previously traveled to the Holy Land and have stood at this site, what are your memories?

Now that you have actually stood at the Jordan River, do you see this story of the baptism of Jesus in a different light?

For those who are thinking about a visit to the Holy Land, pray and ask God to provide the time and means for you to experience this special location.

For additional information, visit http://www.seetheholyland.net.

Mount of Beatitudes

RECORD YOUR STUDY resources here.

Usually on the second or third day of each of my trips to Israel, I have visited the Mount of Beatitudes. Located in the northwestern area of the Sea of Galilee, near Capernaum and Tabgha, crowds of men, women, and children heard the message Jesus preached, now referred to as the Sermon on the Mount. A beautiful octagonal-shaped church marks the site where some of Jesus's most familiar words were spoken. The church was built in 1937 and is administered by the Catholic Church.

Locate the Mount of Beatitudes on a map of Israel. Get your camera ready. This beautiful site, overlooking the farmlands and orchards that line the western coast of the Sea of Galilee, is part of the land allotted to the tribe of Naphtali.

Most tour groups will stand on the patio of the church overlooking the Sea of Galilee to read Matthew 5:1–16, the Beatitudes.

Stop!

Read Matthew 5:1–16 as the primary text. (The entire sermon continues on through the end of 8:5.) As you read, ask yourself if this message is still relevant for today.

Note words you might want to research. For instance, what does "blessed" mean?

As a general overview, read 5:17–48. Write out verse 48.

Look!

Research the words you listed in the Stop! section.

The word "blessed" in these verses can be understood as the people who were blessed by God. *Blessed* means "a divine joy."

Verses 3–10 may sound like a list of rituals or works, but this is not so. These verses describe personal character traits that should be seen by the unbelieving world, in the lives of every Christian.

Note that verses 3, 10, and 20 refer to "the kingdom of Heaven" rather than the kingdom of God. Why? Remember that the author of this book was Jewish and was writing primarily to convince the Jews that Jesus was the promised Messiah. Jews seldom write out the name *God* in reverence to Him. Matthew used the phrase "kingdom of Heaven" to avoid writing out the name *God*.

Matthew was also sure to record the strong language Jesus had for the scribes and Pharisees. As you read this, you will see that Jesus was making a basic point: it's about your righteousness and not about works and rituals.

Verse 20 seems to describe the key point of this sermon. Write out this verse.

Jesus also sought to expand the understanding of the people and the religious leaders of six points of the law. These six topics are not deep doctrine (though they are discussed in the Ten Commandments), but they are important aspects of day-to-day living. All of the people listening would not only have been able to understand what Jesus was saying, but they were also able to apply these to their individual lives.

Describe what each of the following sets of verses speaks about:

Verses 21–26

Verses 27–30

Verses 31–32

Verses 33–37

Verses 38–42

Verses 43–47

According to verse 20, what is the purpose of this sermon?

According to verses 21–47, how can this be applied to life?

Though we are not focusing on chapters 6–7, these chapters are part of the Sermon on the Mount and include the Lord's Prayer (in chapter 6), and the familiar words "judge not that you be not judged" (7:1).

Matthew 5:14 also describes us as "the light of the world, a city on a hill [that] cannot be hidden." Scholars believe that Jesus was using an object lesson by pointing out something that would have been easy for the people to see, as was his custom. The Jewish city of Safed is a few miles to the northeast of the site of this sermon. Perhaps it was dusk or twilight, and Jesus was pointing out the lights of the city. Find Safed on a map of the Sea of Galilee.

As Jesus left this site, He traveled to Capernaum (Matt. 8:5). You will see Capernaum on this trip! (We will save a study of Capernaum for Volume 2.)

Listen!
Summarize what God was trying to teach us through the sermon of Jesus.

What if this Sermon had been left out of Scripture?

How can you apply this lesson to the following areas of your life today?

At your work?

At home, with family, and spouse?

At you read the headlines in the news?

Your desires and wants?

As you plan your ministry to the Lord?

For additional information, go to http://www.seetheholyland.net.

The Gates of Jerusalem

RECORD YOUR STUDY resources here.

Stop!
Why study the gates of a city?

Gates are mentioned many times in scripture. You may read over the word "gate" but never think much about it. If you can, find a *Strong's Concordance* and look up all the references to gates in scripture.

What do you know about the gates of Jerusalem?

On a trip to Jerusalem, you will walk through a number of gates that are mentioned in scripture, as well as other modern, historically significant gates.

There are significant gates in the Galilee. If you go to the ancient city of Dan, you will see the ruins of the city gate that Abraham probably walked through as he entered the city to rescue Lot. When you go to Megiddo, you will walk through the ancient gates leading into the ruins of the city.

One day, Jesus will return for His own and enter through the Golden (Eastern) Gate.

Gates were not only for protection, permitting only friendly people to pass in and out while barring the enemies from storming the city, but gates were used as a place of business, civic activities, and judicial action. Made of steel and wood, gates were opened during the day and closed at sunset.

When Nehemiah returned to Jerusalem, one of his first projects was to get the people to repair the gates and walls of the city (Nehemiah 2 and 3). Why?

Gates were usually named for their function or location. For example, the Dung Gate led to the garbage dump of the city, and the Flower Gate was the entrance to the flower market.

Several gates were named for distant cities. For example, the Damascus Gate led to the road travelers used to travel north to Damascus, Syria. The Jaffa Gate led to the road travelers took to Jaffa, a city on the coast.

Let's study a number of the gates of Jerusalem in the land allocated to the tribes of Benjamin and Judah.

Look!
Note the activity taking place at the gates of the city in the following verses.

2 Sam. 15:2
2 Chron. 32:6
Gen. 19:1
Isa. 29:1
1 Kings 21:10

Read the verses and summarize the information about each gate. You will see and walk through some of these gates!

Golden Gate, also known as the Eastern Gate or Beautiful Gate (Ezek. 43:4; Acts 3:2, 3:10; Zech. 14:15; Neh. 3:29; Josh. 12:12–15). You will not walk through this gate.

Dung Gate, or Potsherd Gate (Neh. 2:13, 3:14, 12:31)—This is the gate closest to the site most holy to the Jewish religion, the Wailing Wall, or Western Wall. It is located on the southern wall of the city. You will probably walk through this gate.

Lions' Gate, also known as Stephen's Gate or Sheep Gate (Acts 6:8–15, 7:54–60; Neh. 3:1, 32; John 5:2)—This gate is on the eastern side of the city wall, north of the Golden Gate. You will walk through this gate. It is called Lions' Gate for the two images of lions that are engraved on the doorposts to the gate, and called Stephen's Gate because Stephen, of the books of Acts, was taken through this gate to be martyred outside the city, It is also known as the Sheep Gate because sheep were brought through this gate to the temple for sacrifice.

Damascus Gate, or Nablus Gate. This gate is located at the middle of the northern wall of Jerusalem. This is the gate Jesus probably walked through carrying His cross to Golgotha. Today it is probably the busiest gate, with markets and community activities taking place in this area. You will walk through this gate on the way to the Garden Tomb.

Other gates mentioned in scripture include the following:

Water Gate (Neh. 3:26)

Fish Gate (Neh. 3:3). This gate was located on northwest corner of city wall. Fishermen from the coast would enter this gate to bring fish to the city.

Valley Gate (Neh. 2:13, 2:15, 3:13)

Horses Gate (Neh. 3:28)

The following gates were not mentioned in scripture:

Herod's Gate, or Flower Gate. This gate is on the northwest corner of the city wall and is a few feet north of the Damascus Gate.

Zion Gate. Built in 1540, this gate is important in modern history and played a role in the 1967 war to retake the city of Jerusalem. The Israeli Defense Forces made one of the major entrances into the city through this gate. Even today, bullet holes can be seen around the outside of this gate, which is located on the southwest corner of the Western Wall on Mount Zion. You will walk through this gate. This gate is also called the Wounded Gate because of the bullet holes.

Jaffa Gate. This is a modern gate. It was built in 1538 on the Western Wall of Jerusalem.

Other important gate references include the following:
    Jesus referred to Himself as "The Gate" in John 10:9.

Revelation 21 mentions twelve gates.

Listen!
Summarize what God has taught you through this lesson.

Which gate was most interesting to you?

Get your cameras ready; you will be busy taking photos of some of these gates!

Stop and pray, thanking God for this trip!

For additional information, go to http://www.seetheholyland.net.

6

The Church of Saint Peter in Gallicantu

RECORD YOUR STUDY resources here.

Saint Peter in Gallicantu is an impressive and memorable site. It is located on a hill overlooking Jerusalem, the Kidron Valley, the Mount of Olives, and the Garden of Gethsemane. A rich man, like the high priest Caiaphas, would have acquired this prime real estate. The site is located in Jerusalem on land allocated to the tribes of Benjamin and Judah.

After touring this beautiful church, you will walk down narrow, dark, dank steps leading into what archaeologists believe were dungeons under the house of the high priest during the time of Jesus. This is probably where Jesus was held overnight after his arrest in the Garden of Gethsemane, before he was sent to Pontius Pilate. On one exterior wall of the church is a beautiful mosaic depicting Jesus being lowered down into the dungeon or pit.

Stop!
Read and study the story of Jesus (Mark 14:53–65; Matt. 26:57, 59–68; Luke 22:54, 63-71: John 18:12-14, 19-24, 28.)

Jesus spent the night at the home of the high priest (Matt. 27:1–2; Luke 22:66; Josh. 18:28), which enforces the idea that He was held in one of the dungeons.

This is also the site where Peter denied Jesus three times. You will see a courtyard with a beautiful sculpture depicting Peter with the slave girl as he denied Jesus three times. On the pinnacle of the church over the cross is an image of a rooster (the word *Gallicantu* is Latin for "rooster").

Read and study the story of Peter (John. 18:15–18, 25–27; Mark 14:54, 66–72; Matt. 26:58, 69–75; Luke 22:54–62).

Look!
Now a surprise.

I first found Psalm 88 at Saint Peter of Gallicantu. I know I had read over the Psalms several times, but I had never understood the meaning of Psalm 88 the way I was about to understand it.

As we stood in a deep pit far below the floors of the church, the pastor read Psalm 88. We could imagine the scene as the pastor spoke. Jesus would have been bound and lowered into one of these holding chambers. It was dark and isolated, just as it would have been when Jesus was kept prisoner. As the pastor read this psalm, we thought of Jesus. Many of us shed tears as we stood there and could imagine how terrible it must have been for Jesus.

Read Psalm 88 while imagining Jesus in a deep, cold, dirty pit. Imagine the darkness. Picture Jesus alone, knowing what He would face in the hours to follow. Not only was He a prisoner, but His friends (except Peter, who will be discussed later) had all deserted Him.

What phrases do you see in Psalm 88 that might apply to Jesus? Is this a prophecy? Perhaps this psalm was given by God, not only as a prayer, but as a prophecy of the Suffering Servant.

Listen!

You will stand in a pit at the house of the high priest. You will somewhat sense what Jesus was going through. What is God saying to you through Psalm 88?

How can you apply Psalm 88 to the following areas of your life today?

At work?

At home, with family, and spouse?

As you read the headlines in the news?

As you plan your ministry to the Lord?

Stop and pray.

For additional information, go to http://www.seetheholyland.net.

7

The Jesus Boat
(The Ancient Boat)

RECORD YOUR STUDY resources here.

In 1986, at the peak of a season of drought, two Israeli brothers found the remains of an ancient boat along the shore of the Sea of Galilee. After contacting the Israeli Antiquities Department, the major task was undertaken to bring this boat, intact, out of the deep mud in which it was encased.

With the tools of modern technology, the ancient boat was raised. It is now housed in the Yigal Alon Museum, which is operated by Kibbutz Ginosar. The first time I saw the boat was in 1991, when it was housed in a small, makeshift, climate-controlled tin building. Now the museum is a modern, high-class building with a full tourist shop and a small deli. Most tourist groups to the Galilee will stop at this site.

Despite scientific carbon dating to indicate that the wood is probably from the time of Jesus, the Jesus Boat Center never claims that this is the actual boat that Jesus or the disciples used on the Sea of Galilee, but we can use our imagination—and when we get to Heaven, we can ask Jesus if the boat at Yigal Alon Museum was one of His boats!

The ancient boat has a variety of types of wood and appears to have been patched up over its years of use. It would hold fifteen people. It was twenty-seven feet long, 7.5 feet wide, and 4.3 feet high.

This study will remind you of one of the several episodes of Jesus, water, and boats. He walked on water. He caused an unexpected large catch of fish. He stilled the storm. He called the fishermen. He stood in a boat and preached to the people on the shore.

The eastern coast of the Sea of Galilee is located in the land allocated to the tribes of Naphtali and Zebulum (depending on your reference map).

Let's focus on Jesus in the boat as he calmed the storm.

You will ride on a boat on the Sea of Galilee. This is a highlight of the trip, and very seldom does a tour group miss this outing. There are many sites that we are not sure are original. We call them *traditional* sites. The Sea of Galilee is the Sea of Galilee of the time of Jesus. When you are on a boat on the Sea of Galilee, it is the exact Sea of Galilee spoken of in scripture. There is no doubt about this site.

Stop!

Read and summarize Mark 4:35–41. (Other stories of Jesus and boats/ water are found in Matthew 8:23–27, Luke 8:22–26, and Matthew 14:19–28.)

John does not report these events, as the other Gospels report, yet he was usually with Jesus, and was probably in the boat at this event. Luke was not present, yet he reported the event. Mark might have been present. Matthew might have been present.

Mark 4:36 notes that other little boats were with them. What happened to them?

The word "but," which contrasts and compares, is recorded twice. What is the purpose of what is being contrasted in Mark 4:38?

What is being contrasted in Mark 4:40?

Look!

Consider the following example of deep study.

I always study familiar words to make sure I know what scripture is saying to us. For this study, I looked up the words "asleep" (# 2518) and "storm" (# 2978) in a Strong's Concordance, and a Word Study Dictionary. I wanted to know what kind of sleep and what kind of storm were implied.

I found that the word "storm" refers to a whirlwind, hurricane, or tempest (not just a little rain and wind). The word "sleep" refers to being fully asleep (not dozing).

Jesus, the creator of the Sea of Galilee, knew there was going to be a storm. He created the storm. Why would He have made the disciples go through this?

What did the disciples learn?

Does God put you in the middle of storms to teach you something about life and about Him? How? Why?

If the boat could speak, what might it say?

Listen!

How can you apply this story of Jesus calming the storm to the following areas of your life today?

At work?

At home, with family, and spouse?

As you read the headlines in the news?

In your ministry to the Lord?

Stop, pray, and thank God for this opportunity to see His Holy Land!

For additional information, go to http://www.seetheholyland.net.

8

Chorazin

Record your study resources here.

We don't visit Chorazin often. I visited it once in 1991, and I did not visit it again until 2014.

Someone might say, "It is just a pile of rocks and ruins." Yes, but it has such significance!

Chorazin is just ruins. Birds, small animals, and insects live among the rocks and trees. So what is the big deal? Why study Chorazin?

First of all, Jesus spoke of Chorazin. We study His words.

Second, we see some amazing ruins of ancient days: a synagogue, a home, and other ancient structures.

Third, we see the fulfilment of prophecy in the ruins of Chorazin (and in Capernaum and Bethsaida as well). Jesus said these three cities would be destroyed, and they were.

Why is prophecy important? If Jesus kept His promise about Chorazin, Capernaum, and Bethsaida, we can feel secure that He will keep His other promises—namely, that He will return one day to take believers to be with Him!

Chorazin is located in the land allocated to the tribe of Naphtali.

Stop!
Read Luke 10:10–16.

Mark the words and sentences that explain using the words *because* or *for.*

Find a map of the Sea of Galilee and locate the site of ancient Chorazin.

Look!
What does the word "woe" mean in verse 13?

What are "mighty works" referred to in verse 13?

What does the word "repent" mean in verse 13?

Verse 16 refers to hearing, but this does not mean hearing with the ear. What does this mean?

What is "rejecting" Jesus in verse 16?

What other words might you want to research in this section of scripture?

Now go to Matthew 11:20–24. Stop! and Look! as you did with Luke 10. Summarize any additional information from these verses.

In Matthew 11, we note that just prior to calling down the three cities, Jesus had been chastising the people for not recognizing John the Baptist, and not accepting the forgiveness through the repentance Jesus offered them. Their lack of repentance led to Jesus calling the woe on these three cities, with the resulting judgment and punishment.

Jesus said that Chorazin, Bethsaida, and Capernaum would fall, and they did. These sites were all busy, heavy populated cities during the time of Jesus, but this is no longer so. This is a prophecy fulfilled.

Listen!

Summarize what Jesus taught us through the woes to Chorazin, Bethsaida, and Capernaum.

How can you apply this teaching by Jesus to the following areas of your life today?

   At work?

At home, with family, and spouse?

As you read the headlines in the news?

In your ministry to the Lord?

Stop and pray.

9

Temple Mount

RECORD YOUR STUDY resources here.

One of the most amazing things about a visit to the Holy Land is a visit to the City of God and the Temple Mount. The most holy place in the world! Wow! You are going to stand in Jerusalem at the most holy of places!

In the hustle and bustle of seeing sights and jet lag, sometimes it is easy to take for granted that you are standing on *holy ground*. It has been said that "Israel is the center of the world, Jerusalem is the center of Israel, and the Temple Mount is the center of Jerusalem."

The Temple Mount is in the land allocated to the tribes of Benjamin and Judah.

Stop!
Find the location of Jerusalem on a map of Israel.

Find the location of the Temple Mount on a map of Jerusalem from the time of Jesus.

What do you remember about the history of the Temple Mount during the following periods?

Before the city was built?

When David purchased the area of the Temple Mount?

When and how the temples were built?

When God Himself dwelled with mankind in the temple?

When Jesus (God) walked on the Temple Mount

What the activities of the New Testament took place on the Temple Mount?

Look!

Read the following text. Make note of important words and concepts:

Before the city was built, Abraham was told by God to sacrifice his only son, Isaac, on Mount Moriah. Moriah is the geographical ridge located to the north of the Temple Mount. Read Genesis 22:1–19. Note the building of an altar—a precursor to the sacrificial offerings to take place in the future.

Read 2 Samuel 24:15–25, which is the story of David purchasing the plot of land that would become the Temple Mount from Araunah. Here, David built an altar and presented a sacrifice to the Lord.

Read 2 Chronicles 3:1–2 and 1 Kings 6:1, 6:11–13, and 9:1–5, which describe the building of the first temple by Solomon. Note the words "forever" and "perpetually" in 1 Kings 9:3b. What do these words mean?

The second temple was built by Zerubbabel (Ezra 3, 4, 5) and expanded by Herod.

God Himself was actually present on earth with mankind in the temple. Read Exodus 25:8–9, 25:22, and 40:34–37.

Jesus (God living among men on earth) on the Temple Mount as He worshipped, healed, taught, and forgave. And you will walk in that same area!

Read 2 Samuel 7:4–17. God told David to build Him a place to dwell among the people. God often reviews past history as He makes promises for the future as He does in these verses.

What is meant by "My name" in 2 Samuel 7:13?

Who are the 'My people' in 2 Samuel 7:7, 8, 10 and 11?

Verses 12-17 are not only promises to the King David, but prophecy.

Why would the city of Jerusalem be called the "City of God" (1 Kings 11:36; Ps. 46:4–5; Ps. 48:1)?

Listen!
Why study the Temple Mount?

The Temple Mount is the epicenter of world news today. As students of scripture, it is important for us to understand the history of the Temple Mount to better understand the absence of a Temple today, the presence of the Dome of the Rock and the Mosque standing in the same location as the first and second temples, as well as the events predicted to happen in the future.

The Temple Mount will continue to be the center of worship for major religions today, as well as the center of political unrest, until Jesus comes back!

What have you learned about the Temple Mount from this study that will impact your visit there?

Go to http://www.seetheholyland.net for more information.

10

Caesarea Maritime

RECORD YOUR STUDY resources here.

What do you already know about Caesarea Maritime? Where is it located? What events took place here?

Stop!
Find Caesarea Maritime on a map of Israel. Hint: it is on the coast, located in the area of land allocated to the tribes of Dan and Manasseh.

This coastal city was built by Herod, the builder of the second temple. The heavily populated center for the Roman government included homes, racing tracts, places of worship, a palace with swimming pools built into the ocean, a major seaport, and a large Roman theatre seating thirty-five hundred spectators for entertainment and legal proceedings at the Bema Seat before the throne of the governor.

There are many New Testament events that took place at Caesarea Maritime. The city was named in honor of the Roman Caesar and located on the seacoast, hence, identified with name *Maritime*. (This site is not to be confused with Caesarea Philippi in the north, which is a later study.)

Most tours visit this site. You will stand in the ruins of the theatre that served as the place of judgments pronounced on criminals brought before Herod Agrippa, Felix, and other governmental leaders.

Look!

Study the following events that took place at Caesarea Maritime.

In Acts 9:26–30, God changed Saul's name to Paul after his conversion on the Damascus Road. He went to Jerusalem to join with the church and apostles and was initially rejected by them.

Paul and Cornelius (Acts 10:1–8, 24–48)

King Herod went to Caesarea, spoke before the population, and was struck down by God (Acts 12:18–19, 22–23). This took place in the Roman theatre that is visited by tourists. Why did God kill him (verse 23)?

Home of Philip the Evangelist (Acts 21:8–9)

Herod sends Paul to Caesarea (Acts 23:23–31).

Paul before Agrippa and Drusilla at Caesarea (Acts 24)

In Acts 25–26, Paul speaks of Jesus before Felix and Bernice at Caesarea. Acts 26:28 records Felix stating that he was almost convinced by Paul that Jesus was the Messiah.

At this site, you will see a replica of the Pilate Stone. In 1962 the Pontius Pilate Stone was discovered, which provides tangible evidence of Pilate's presence in Judea during Jesus's time. It also gives clarification of his title. This is more evidence that the Bible is true and not just a collection of myths.

Listen!

If you have visited Caesarea, what do you remember about the sights and sounds?

Paul spoke up in defense of the Lord Jesus at the risk of his own life. How does apply to the following areas of your life today?

At work?

At home?

At church?
In your ministry to the LORD?

Go to http://www.bibleworks.com for photographs of Caesarea and http://www.seetheholyland.net for more information about this site.

11

Caesarea Philippi
(Banias)

RECORD YOUR STUDY resources here.

Stop!
Find Caesarea Philippi on a map of Israel. It is located in the far north of Galilee.

Over the centuries, this spot has also been known as Banias, Banyas, and Panias.

Do you remember the story of Jesus speaking about the gates of Hell? Do you remember when Peter confessed that Jesus was the Christ? Both events took place at Caesarea Philippi. You will visit the site where Jesus spoke these words, and you will see the "Gates of Hell."

For general information, read Matthew 16:13–20 and Mark 8:27–30. This is a beautiful area in northern Galilee. This area was not mentioned in the Old Testament but was in the area allotted to the tribe of Dan. During the time of Jesus, this area was heavily populated because of the abundant water supply and cool temperatures in the summer months. It was named after the Caesar.

Look!

In ancient Greek, the letters *P* and *B* are interchangeable. Therefore, the Greek name for this site is Panias or Banias. The cave of the god Pan was the site of ritual human sacrifices that took place at a rock crevice known as the Gates of Hell. This may have been a visual object lesson when Jesus spoke here and said, "the Gates of Hell shall not prevail."

The waters flowing from Mount Hermon provide the majority of the water supply for Israel, and the outflow is seen here at the foot of the mountain. Lush green areas near abundant water and fertile ground made this a logical place for families to make their homes. This would have been prime real estate for the rich. King Agrippa II built a palace here. This general area is also called the Hermon Reserve and the Dan Nature Reserve.

Caesarea Philippi is located in the land allotted to the tribe of Dan in the north. Although the tribe of Dan had been allocated land on the coast, it could never overthrow the Canaanites living there, so it relocated to this northern area.

Study Matthew 16:13–20 and Mark 8:27–30.

Why would Jesus ask, "Who do men say that I am?" (Matthew 16 states that Jesus identified Himself as the "Son of Man")

Why would people think that Jesus was the return of John the Baptist?

Why would people think that Jesus was the return of Elijah?

Why would people think that Jesus was the return of Jeremiah?

Peter answered, "You are the Christ." What is "the Christ"?

Why would Jesus tell the disciples not to tell anyone? In Mark 8, He "strictly warned them."

Jesus spoke of the gates of Hell while standing next to an opening in the cliffs known as the Gates of Hell. Pagans who worshipped in this area believed that the opening led to Hell, and may have thrown men, women and children into the crevice as offerings to the gods. Jesus may have pointed to this rock formation as He spoke.

Matthew 16:18 is the first time the word "church" is mentioned in scripture. The word *church* in Greek means "the called-out ones."

Listen!

You will visit Caesarea Philippi.

What was the importance of this event to Peter, to Jesus, and to us?

What can you use from the teachings of Jesus at Caesarea Philippi in your life today?

Summarize the event at Caesarea Philippi.

Stop and thank God for your trip to the Holy Land.

See http://www.seetheholyland.net for further information.

Mount Tabor

RECORD YOUR STUDY resources here.

MOUNT TABOR IS best known for the story of Deborah and Barak. Located in the Jezreel Valley, it is six miles east of Nazareth and eleven miles west of the Sea of Galilee. It served as a boundary point between the tribes of Issachar, Naphtali, and Zebulun. Mount Tabor is shaped like an upside-down bowl—very easy to identify.

As a boy, Jesus would have been familiar with Mount Tabor. He grew up within sight of it. As a Jewish boy, Jesus knew the story of the great battle between God's people and Sisera, a Canaanite king during the time of the judges. Perhaps Jesus and his friends even adventured to Tabor and climbed to the top.

Some scholars believe that Mount Tabor was the location of the Transfiguration, although others believe that Mount Hermon was the more likely site.

What do you already know about Deborah, Barak, and the battle in the Jezreel Valley? There was another woman in this story. Can you name her?

Deborah was the first (and only) female judge of Israel. She did not rule the nation, but she gave the people and the nation godly advice.

Stop!
Locate Mount Tabor on a map.

Read Judges 4 and 5 as a quick general overview.

Look for words that explain the story using words such as *because, for,* and *so that.*

Look!
Read the verses again.

Deborah was the first and only female judge of Israel. Summarize the role of a judge (Judg. 2:16–19).

Deborah's role as judge seemed different from the role of a male judge. Some call Deborah the first female army general. Who was the leader? Who was the follower? What was the role of Barak? What was the role of Deborah? Write the key words from the following verses.

4:4
4:5
4:6
4:8
4:14
4:15
4:16
4:22
5:1
5:7
5:12

Why was this woman given the honor to be the only female judge? What was the spiritual climate at this time? Where was the male leadership? What were the circumstances in the nation that there was no man assigned as a judge at this time? Read the last verse of the book of Judges.

Deborah was a judge and also a prophetess. What is a prophetess? Were the duties of a prophetess similar to those of a male prophet? Think of male prophets, such as Jeremiah, Obadiah, Joel, and Ezekiel, and compare their roles to the role of Deborah.

God never again assigned the role of a judge to a woman. What was so special about Deborah that she received this honor? Where were the godly men at that time who could have been judges?

What does the prophet Isaiah say about a country ruled by a woman? (Isa. 3:12)

Deborah prophesized to Barak that the glory for the battle would be given to a woman. Which woman? (Some have nicknamed this women "the little woman with a big hammer.")

Listen!

What would we have missed out on if this story had been left out of scripture? Was it important for us to know about this particular battle? About Deborah and Barak?

Notice Deborah's approach to Barak. She was not aggressive or overly assertive. She was an advisor and a good follower. How do her actions/attitudes transfer over to the world around us today?

What lessons have you learned from Deborah that you can apply to your life today?

See http://www.bibleplaces.com or http://www.seetheholyland.net for more information.

13

Megiddo
(Armageddon)

RECORD YOUR STUDY resources here.

Locate the site of the ruins of Megiddo, or Armageddon, on a map of Israel. It is in the land allocated to the tribe of Issachar.

Megiddo is a name that is familiar to most people. The first thought is usually of Armageddon, as it is the site of the preparation of the great army of the kings of the east in the days of the tribulation. But there is so much more to Megiddo.

Review Revelation 16:16, which describes the great army in the valley of Armageddon. Most people are very interested in Armageddon. For this study we will not focus on end-time events, but will study the other scripture that mentions this Megiddo/Armageddon.

Summarize what you know about other events (besides those in the book of Revelation) that took place at Megiddo.

Is this site mentioned in any other scriptures of the New Testament?

Stop!

Because of the location of Megiddo, it was much-coveted real estate. It is located above the Jezreel Valley, along the major trade route of the Via Maris. All the nations north of Israel wanted to control this site. Archaeological digs show evidence of seven layers of civilization; seven different populations existed at the site for a period of time. Each civilization was overthrown by enemies who rebuilt the city upon the previous layer. The prime reason for any city to exist is its location. The location must provide security, water, and food. Megiddo had all three.

Over the centuries, battles were fought, and kings were killed and buried at Megiddo.

This is the area of the tribe of Manasseh.

Look!

What do you find in these verses?

Josh. 12:21
Josh. 17:11 and 1 Chron. 7:29
Judg. 1:27
Judg. 5:19
1 Kings 4:7–8, 4:12
1 Kings 9:10–15
2 Kings 9:27
2 Kings 23:29–30 and 1 Chron. 35:22
Zech. 12:1–11 (Verse 11 is key. This is an end-times prophecy.)

Visitors today will visit Tel Megiddo and look out over the Jezreel Valley. It is easy to imagine millions of soldiers of the kings of the east gathering in the valley below. On a clear day, you can see all the way to Mount Tabor in the west.

Listen!

What would you have missed out on if you had not studied all these verses in the Old Testament about Megiddo?

Can you apply any of this to your life today?

Stop and pray, thanking God that you will get an opportunity to visit this amazing and important site.

See http://www.bibleplaces.com or http://www.seetheholyland.net for more information.

Pool of Bethesda

RECORD YOUR STUDY resources here.

Find the location of the Pool of Bethesda on a map of Jerusalem.

What do you remember about the miracle healing by Jesus at the Pool of Bethesda?

This site is located within a short walk to the Lions' Gate, which opens on the eastern side of the city wall. There is a beautiful courtyard with colorful, blooming flowers (when they are in season). The ruins of the pool may surprise you. They are below where you will stand. Over the centuries, building has gone on around this site, moving the pools below street level.

Adjacent to the ruins of the pool is the beautiful Crusader church named the Church of Saint Anne. Anne was the mother of Mary, the mother of Jesus. Tradition indicates that this site was the home of Anne.

This church is not just another church to visit. It is the church where groups stop to sing praises to the Lord. Often there are several groups of tourists awaiting entrance. The construction of the church causes sound waves to rebound off the walls, resulting in the most beautiful sounds. This is the site where everyone sings. No one ever forgets that moment. I often wonder how many thousands—if not millions—of tourists have stopped to sing at this site in every language in the world!

Stop!
Read John 5:1–18 as a general overview.

You will stand in the place where this miracle took place. There is little doubt that these are the same pools mentioned in John 5.

Look!
Read John 5:1–8 again. Study it this time.

You will walk through the same Lions Gate if you enter from the east.

Jesus took the initiative to heal this man by reaching out and speaking to him.

Besides the healing, what else is of importance? What was the outcome?

Jesus healed this man, and His enemies went wild! This was another one of those events that pointed Jesus to the cross. His enemies, the religious leaders, never believed that Jesus was the Messiah.

Listen!
You will stand at the ruins of the Pool of Bethesda. Jesus was there. Jesus spoke. Jesus healed. Jesus brought the wrath of the religious community against Him.

Thank God for the opportunity to visit this special site!

Visit http://www.seetheholyland.net for pictures of this site.

Appendix

The Most Important Thing

Do you know for sure that you are a child of God and that you will spend eternity in Heaven with Jesus?

As my testimony recounts, I was baptized at the age of ten and thought I was a Christian. I was a child and had no real idea about what being baptized meant. I was not saved. I was not a follower of Jesus. I was headed for an eternity separated from God. I became a child of God years later at the age of forty-two.

Rededicate your life this very day. Take a moment and go to God in prayer. Talk to God and go through all the steps of the sinner's prayer.

Jesus, I know I am a sinner.
I believer that You died for me and took my sins upon Yourself.
Thank You for dying on the cross for me.
I dedicate my life to You and will follow You all my days.
I am Your child!

If you believe the words you have just prayed, then this is an important day; it is your day of salvation or rededication. Happy birthday! This is your new spiritual birthday! Write the date here:_____
_____

Overview of the Stop! Look! Listen! Bible Study Technique

For a complete explanation of this method of study, see the book *Bible Study Basics: Stop! Look! Listen! A Do-It-Yourself Bible Study Technique.*

Always record the resources you use during your study.

Stop! General Overview

Pray before you begin.

1. Ask yourself the following questions: Why I am studying this topic or book? What do I already know? Where does this event take place?

2. Who is the author? Why did he or she write it?

3. Read the entire chapter or book for general information and an overview. Read slowly and purposefully. Read every word.

4. Stop! When God explains something, words such as *because, for,* and *so that* are used.

5. Pick out key words and concepts that you do not understand. Make a list. You will research these words in the Look! section.

6. Scan the horizon. Where does this take place? Is geography important? God mentions the geographical location very often. If it is important to Him, it must be important to us.

Look! Research

Read the chapter or book again, this time to gain information and see what God is saying.

1. Research the study words and concepts from the Stop! section.

2. What are the key points and theme?

3. Look left! Look right! What came before? What came after?

4. Ask questions. Answer questions. Make charts as necessary.

Listen!

1. Read the verses again.

2. Always ask yourself, "Why did God give us this story?"

3. What if this story had been left out of scripture?

4. How do I apply this story to my life today?

5. Pray.

For a complete explanation of the SLL method, see the book *Bible Study Basics: Stop! Look! Listen! A Do-It-Yourself Bible Study Technique* by this author.

Post-Trip Quiz
Israel in the World

How long would it take you to locate Israel on a world map?

Name the oceans and seas bordering Israel (not including the Dead Sea).

Name the country south of Israel.

Name the countries east of Israel.

Name the countries north of Israel.

What is the capital of Israel as observed by the major nations of the world?

What is the capital of Israel as designated by the Israeli government?

Post-Trip Quiz
Geography of the Land

Draw the basic outline of Israel. Label the following:

1. Mediterranean Sea
2. Sea of Galilee
3. Jordan River
4. Dead Sea
5. Jerusalem
6. Capernaum
7. Bethlehem
8. Nazareth
9. Any other locations you have learned about on your trip.

Be sure to add the countries of Jordan, Egypt, Syria, and Lebanon.

Post-Trip Quiz
Geography of the Sea of Galilee

The Sea of Galilee was the location of many of the miracles of Jesus. Draw the basic outline of the Sea of Galilee. Locate and label the following:

1. Tiberias
2. Migdol
3. Capernaum
4. Site of Sermon on the Mount
5. Golan Heights
6. Site of the feeding of the multitude
7. Site of the healing of the demoniac man (swine into sea)
8. Inlet of water into the Sea of Galilee
9. The outflow site into the Jordan River

Just think: at the conclusion of your trip, you will know where these sites are located!

Dig Deeper: Additional Sites to Study

Bethlehem—Story of Ruth and the birth of Jesus	Ruth, Luke 2
Capernaum—Daughter of Jairus raised	Mark 5:21–24, 36–43; Luke 8:41–42
Capernaum—Jesus and the woman with the issue of blood	Mark 5:25–34; Luke 8:43–48
Capernaum—Jesus heals Peter's mother-in-law.	Luke 4:38–39
Capernaum—Jesus heals the centurion's son.	Luke 7:1–10
Dead Sea—Lot and family	Genesis 19
Ein Gedi—David and King Saul	2 Sam. 23:29–24:25
Eilat—Queen of Sheba visits Solomon.	1 Kings 10:1–13
Jerusalem—David and Abigail	1 Sam. 25
Jerusalem—Athaliah, the only queen of Israel	2 Kings 11
Jerusalem—David and Bathsheba	2 Sam. 11–12
Jerusalem—Peter and Rhoda, the servant girl	Acts 12:12–18
Jaffa—Peter and Dorcas (or Tabitha)	Acts 9:36–42
Jordan River—Healing of Naaman	2 Kings 5:1–14
Jerusalem—David and wife Michal	1 Sam. 19:11–18
Jericho—The Israelites enter the Promised Land.	Josh. 2
Nain—Jesus raises a widow's son.	Luke 7:11–16
Nazareth—Jesus, Mary, and Joseph	Luke 1, 2
Samaria—Jesus and the Samaritan woman	John 4
Temple Mount—Adulterous woman is forgiven.	John 8:1–12
Temple Mount—The women with the two mites	Luke 21:1–4
Temple Mount—Dedication of baby Jesus	Luke 2:21–38

Additional Information on the Internet

All Things Jewish	http://www.askmoses.com
Bible Places	http://www.bibleplaces.com
Global Jewish Advocacy	http://www.ajc.org
Judaism 101—basics of Judaism	http://www.jewfaq.org
Center for Policy Analysis on Palestine	http://www.cprs-palestine.org
Moriah Christian Tours	http://www.moriahtours.com
Israeli Defense Force **	http://www.idf.il
Israeli Ministry of Tourism— information office	http://www.goisrael.com
Israeli Government	http://www.info.gov.il.org
Israel News Agency	http://www.israelpr.com
Israel Ministry of Foreign Affairs	http://www.mfa.gov.il

Jerusalem Post   http://www.jpost.com
(daily online newspaper) **

Jerusalem Center for Public Affairs**   http://www.jcpa.org

Jewish focus—history, definitions, etc.   http://www.askmoses.com

World of the Temple—   http://www.templeinstitute.com
Jewish temple rebuilding program

Jewish Report   http://www. jrep.com

Palestine Authority   http://www.pna.net

See the Holy Land—   http://www.seetheholyland.net
articles and pictures of tourist sites

Western Wall (live cam)   http://www.westernwall.com

Temple Institute   http://www.templeinstitute.com

** Indicates up-to-the-minute news and issues

Bibliography

(ed.) "2006 Digs." *Biblical Archaeology Review* 32, no. 1 (2006): 28–33.

http://www.wikipidia.com

http://www.bibleplaces.com

Boochny, Etty. *The Holy Land: Follow the Steps of Jesus.* Bnei Brak: Stimatzky Ltd., 1999.

Bowosky, Oded. "In The Path of Sennacherib." *Bible Archaeology Review* 31, no. 2 (2005): 24–35.

Cole, Dan P. *The Archaeology of Jerusalem; from David to Jesus. Learners Guide from the video course of the same name by Hershel Hanks.* Biblical Archaeology Society, 1995.

Crown-Tamir, Hela. *How to Walk in the Footsteps of Jesus and the Prophets.* New York: Gefen Books Publishing, 2000.

Eshel, Hanan, Jodi Magness, and Eli Shenhav. "Surprises at Yattir." *Bible Archeology Review* 27, no. 4 (2001): 32–36.

Friedman, Jack. *The Jerusalem Book of Quotations.* Jerusalem: Gefen Publishing House, 2007.

Gitin, Seymour. "Excavating Ekron." *Bible Archaeology Review* 13, no. 6 (2005): 40–56.

Jacobson, David. "Herod's Roman Temple." *Bible Archeology Review* 28, no. 2 (2002): 19–33.

Keller, Werner. *The Bible as History*. 2nd ed. New York: William Morrow & Co., 1981.

King, Philip J. "Why Lacish Matters." *Biblical Archaeology Review* 31, no. 4 (2005): 59–61.

Levitt, Zola. *Jerusalem Forever*. Dallas: Zola Levitt Ministries Inc., 2002.

Levitt, Zola. *The Promised Land*. Dallas: Zola Levitt Ministries Inc., n.d.

Mason, Steven, and Jerome Murphy-O'Conor. "Where Jesus Was Born." *Bible Archeology Review* 14, no. 1 (2000): 31–45.

Mazar, Amihai, and John Camp. "Will Tel Rehov Save the United Monarchy?" *Biblical Archaeology Review* 24, no. 2 (2000): 38–41.

Miller, Stephen M. *Who's Who and Where's Where in the Bible*. Uhrichsville: Barbour Publishing, 2004.

Moeller, Lennart. *The Exodus Case*. Copenhagen: Scandinavia Publishing House, 2002.

Murphy-O'Connor, Jerome. *The Holy Land*. New York: Oxford University Press, 2000.

Nun, Mindel. "Ports of Galilee." *Biblical Archaeology Review* 25, no. 4 (1999).

Oshri, Aviran. "Where Was Jesus Born?" *Archaeology* 58, no. 6 (2005): 42–45.

Pawson, David. *Unlocking the Bible*. Harper Collins Publishers, 2007.

Peterson, Henry L. "Shechem." *Biblical Illustrator.* (1988): 54–55.

Reich, Ronny. "They Are Ritual Baths." *Biblical Archaeology Review* 28, no. 2 (2002): 50–55.

Shanks, Hershel. "Dig Now 2000." *Bible Archeology Review* 28, no. 1 (2002): 18–33.

Smith, Marsha A. Ellis. *Holeman Book of Biblical Chart.* Nashville: Broadman and Holeman, 1993.

Strong, James. *Strong's Exhaustive Concordance of the Bible.* Iowa Falls: World Bible Publishers, n.d.

Varner, William. *Jacob's Dozen's.* Bellmawr: Friends of Israel Gospel Ministry, Inc., 1987.

Wagner, Clarence. *Fascinating Facts about Israel.* Green Forest: New Leaf Press, 2006.

About the Author

JEANNE IS A graduate of the University of New Mexico (BSN), National University (MEd), Harvest Institute for Biblical Studies (MRS), and Covington Theological Seminary (D.Min).

She has been an adjunct professor at the Harvest Institute for Biblical Studies and has taught a Sunday school or Bible study group almost continually since she became a Christian in 1987.

Jeanne has made mission trips to Wales, Kenya, and India. She has made over twenty Bible study trips to Israel and has traveled extensively all over the world.

After serving twenty years as a registered nurse in the US Navy, Jeanne left nursing to focus her life on service to the Lord in a local church setting.

If you ask her about her hobbies, she will answer, "Studying God's word and passing out gospel tracts." If you are in the Knoxville, Tennessee, area and find a gospel tract left in a bathroom or on a shelf, it was probably left there by Jeanne Sant!

Personal Testimony

I became a born-again believer on October 6, 1987, at the late age of forty-two. I had been baptized as a child because my mother wanted me to be baptized. But the baptism meant nothing to me. For all the years to follow, I thought I was a child of God and would be going to Heaven. I had no idea that as I lived my life as a worldly woman, I was headed to an eternity separated from God.

I realize now that over the years, I was searching for something to fill my life, and all the time, God was trying to get my attention. To tell all of this would be too lengthy. God finally did get my attention! God gets all the glory for never giving up on me, for forgiving me of all my sins, and for using me in the work of His kingdom.

As a young woman, I wanted a great job, adventure, a good salary, and fun! My father had been in the US Navy for forty years and kept telling me to go into the Navy as a nurse, so I did. I know now that even this choice was from God, as He prepared me for a future of serving Him in leadership, teaching, the love of travel, and so much more.

On September 1, 1987, I arrived on the beautiful island of Guam for a two-year assignment as the head of the operating room. I didn't want that particular job, and I didn't want to be so far from my family and friends. My life was a mess, and I was depressed. I did not want to be away from all that was supportive and familiar in my life. But God had other plans.

God arranged for me to be away from anything giving me support. He directed me away from anything familiar. He directed me away from anything of comfort and toward a divine appointment with Him!

I had been on Guam for a few days and was beginning to make plans to search out the best night spots to have fun and meet handsome men in uniform.

Then a sweet young nurse came to my door and invited me to church. I was bored on Sunday mornings, the Navy chapel was just across the street from my quarters, and I had gone to church once or twice over the years. So to be polite, I said yes.

I attended Sunday service and enjoyed it. On Tuesday nights, I decided to attend the Gospel of John Bible Study.

At the first meeting, something about the study intrigued me, and I wanted more. So for the next few Tuesdays, I went across the street and joined in. During the week, I opened my Bible to study some of the concepts we had discussed during the Bible study.

On October 6, during the Tuesday-night Bible study, we were discussing how the disciples had seen all of the miracles of Jesus and had walked and talked with Him. They often disappointed Him, yet He continued to love them. I made some comment to the group that I just didn't understand how they didn't realize that Jesus was God, despite all the time they spent with Him. The disciples just didn't 'get it.'

One of the ladies responded, "Jeanne, it is just like Revelation 3:20: 'Behold, I stand at the door and knock. If anyone hears my voice and opens the door, I will come into them.'" She continued, "Just like with the disciples, Jesus is always with us, trying to get our attention, and we just ignore Him, but He keeps on trying."

For me, that was the exact moment I was born again. It was as if it were something I had always been waiting for, and it had just been dumped in my lap. It was as if a light had come on in a dark room. That was my moment to understand that Jesus loved me, and despite my sinful life, He had been trying to get my attention for a very long time. I got it!

From that exact moment until this exact moment that I type the words on this page, my life has never been the same. I knew God loved me and had a purpose for me if I would just commit to following Him.

A few days later, I was baptized. And a few weeks later, I started to lead my first group for ladies! I realized within a few days that I needed to be studying scripture and meeting with mature, Christian woman. I had so much to learn! I hungered for the word! At our small Navy chapel, we did not have Sunday school or any women's Bible study groups. I needed to be around Christian women!I asked several of the ladies if they were interested in getting together for a Bible study. Surprisingly, ladies who had been Christians for over twenty years said, "You lead it, Jeanne." Wow! I do not recommend asking any new Christian to lead a group or take a major leadership role, but if I wanted a group, I had to lead it myself!

My need for a group outweighed my good sense, so I said OK. That was the beginning of it all!

I left Guam, and the Navy, after two years, and I joined a church in San Diego, California. At my first meeting with the pastor, I mentioned that I had been leading a women's group in Guam. I also told him that I was a new Christian. I was not looking to lead any group.

The pastor had a different idea. The next Sunday, I was leading a large group of men and women! Again, I think this is a dangerous thing to do. I was a new Christian, new to the congregation, and I was leading a group. The pastor knew nothing about me or my theology! Even now, I would not lead a group that included men unless I were sure God wanted me to do so.

But this was in God's plan. I have been teaching almost every week from the time I started in Guam.

God has richly blessed me with the ability to teach, the love of His word, and some actual professional training over the years. I know He wants me to share some of the truths He has taught me with other women! I continue to grow in my ability to teach, and more importantly, grow closer to our Lord Jesus Christ. To God be the glory!

In 1991 I made what I thought would be my first and only trip to the Holy Land. God had other ideas. He has planted a deep love in my heart for the Holy Land and the Jewish people. I have traveled back again and again, and I have never been bored. I am more excited for each new trip than I was for the previous trip. I want to share the importance of the land and my love for the land with the world.

In 2005 I began to put my notes together to write a book about travel to the Holy Land. This is the result. Finally, God has given me the direction I needed to accomplish this wonderful task.

Jeanne Sant

Additional Studies by the Author
Bible Study Basics: Stop! Look! Listen! A Do-It-Yourself Technique

SLL-DIY Study Coming in 2015: *Answering the Question: Who Is Jesus?*

Visit Samanna Ministry on Facebook and at http://www.biblestudy4women@wordpress.com.

Ordering Information
For additional copies of this book, go to Amazon.com or contact the author at http://www.wostudyhall.gmail.com.

For the free article "Travel Tips for the Holy Land," send a request to http://www.wostudyhall@gmail.com.

Made in the USA
San Bernardino, CA
13 October 2017